If Women Ran the World, Sh*t Would Get Done

If Women
Ran the World
Sh*t Would
Get Done

Celebrating all the wonderful, amazing,
stupendous, inspiring, butt-kicking
things women do.

Shelly Rachanow

Conari Press

First published in 2006 by Conari Press,
an imprint of Red Wheel/Weiser LLC
With offices at:
500 Third Street, Suite 230
San Francisco, CA 94107
www.redwheelweiser.com

ISBN-10: 1-57324-289-6
ISBN-13: 978-1-57324-289-9

Library of Congress Cataloging-in-Publication Data

LCC info available upon request.

Cover and interior design by Maija Tollefson
Typeset in Filosofia and Grotesque
Author photo by Simon Gluckman

Printed in Canada
TCP

10 9 8 7 6 5 4 3 2

For women everywhere (past, present, and future),
for all that you've done and continue to do,
thank you!

Contents

Doing . . . for Our Jobs

Doing . . . for the World

Doing . . . for Ourselves

Foreword

When I first saw this book, I pointed it out to my girlfriend and said, "Ain't that the truth!"

She agreed. If women ran the world, sh*t would get done . . . and without all the macho posturing, pissing contests, and testosterone-driven competitiveness.

This wonderful book by Shelly Rachanow is pro-female without being anti-male. She's not interested in male-bashing—she's committed to female-applauding. Her real-life stories, her personal anecdotes, her opportunities for readers' reflections all make this a little book of butt-kicking, spirit-lifting, laugh-inducing, hug-inspiring wisdom and wit for women everywhere.

Here are some of my favorite parts:

- If women ran the world, "happily ever after" wouldn't require a Y chromosome.
- If women ran the world, there would be a Nobel Prize for Friendship.
- A lifetime membership in the Get Sh*t Done Hall of Fame.
- "I have a brain and a uterus, and I use both."
- Isn't it time you said yes! to all the things you have ever planned for yourself?

If you're a butt-kicking, amazing, creative, talented, multi-tasking woman—this book is for you. Read it and celebrate! You rock!

—BJ Gallagher, author of *Women's Work is Never Done*

The Inspiration for This Book

I'm not an egotistical person, but recently I had an aha! moment.

If women ran the world, sh*t would get done.

It was early morning, and despite a badly sprained lower back, I was scrubbing gobs of gunk off some dishes that had sat in the sink overnight. My ordinarily supportive boyfriend was heading out the door, and I asked him to take out the trash. Standing at the sink cleaning disgusting dinnerware was painful enough; lifting heavy bags of garbage wasn't going to happen that morning. I heard him sigh, looked over, and saw that he was pouting.

"Come on, darling, I've taken the trash out three days in a row."

I stared at him in stunned amazement. After all, he knew how much pain I was in. Did he think I was going to cozy up on the couch, snap my fingers, and make the trash disappear? Was he expecting the trash fairy to come pay us a visit?

As he sulked out the door (with trash bag in hand, I might add), it hit me. Women are amazing. When we see something that needs to be changed, improved, or just plain taken care of, we do just that: we take care of it. Women do for our families, our friends, our jobs, the world, and (with the little time that's left) for ourselves. And we do everything that we do (usually) without complaining, even when doing a pitch-perfect imitation of our two-year-old mid-tantrum would be completely justified.

Margaret Thatcher once said, "If you want anything said, ask a man. If you want something done, ask a woman." I think every woman who's ever lived would agree. I also think it's time we stand up, pat ourselves on the back, crack open a pint of chocolate peanut butter ice cream (or just a pint), and celebrate us!

Margaret Thatcher once said, "If you want anything said, ask a man. If you want something done, ask a woman."

Doing . . . for Our Families

Women do so much to nurture, protect, and heal our families. From the days when we emptied chamber pots, trudged through the snow to the apothecary, and scoped out the local butcher's son as a potential son-in-law, to today, when we clean out an Ernie-and-Bert potty, drive to the pharmacy at 4:00 a.m., and remind our my-life-is-over teenager that she's wonderful even though Joe (or was it Tom?) hasn't called, women are always doing for the people we love, and we're not afraid to use strong language or just-manicured fingernails if required.

Like Shirley MacLaine in the movie *Terms of Endearment*, we'll run around a nurse's station like a banshee screaming, "My daughter is in pain. Give her the shot. Do you understand me? Give my daughter the shot!" without a second thought as to what someone might say or think.

Women do whatever we must to keep our families safe, protected, and loved. We always have. It's what we do.

Things Women Do for Their Families . . .
(Between 7:55 and 8:00 A.M.)

7:55:00	Looks through the laundry hamper for husband's missing blue sock.
7:55:28	Assures teenage daughter that her red top looks *fabulous* with her black miniskirt.
7:55:32	Avoids cringing at shortness of miniskirt. Keeps the peace.
7:55:58	Finds husband's sock stuck inside middle schooler's T-shirt.
7:55:59	Also spots toddler's stuffed tiger, missing for the past week, at the bottom of the laundry hamper.
7:56:22	Answers phone. Follows daughter-approved script for talking to daughter's boyfriend. Keeps the peace.
7:56:43	Helps husband locate paper.
7:56:54	Decides not to remind husband that the paper was exactly where he left it last night.

7:57:02	Tosses middle schooler box of cereal as a not-so-subtle reminder to eat breakfast.
7:57:10	Remembers middle schooler has been feeling ignored. Sits next to him at the breakfast table.
7:57:40	Spots toddler attempting to hang the family dog from the railing with the leash.
7:57:41	Leaps up from the chair (without toppling it) to rescue the dog.
7:58:02	Lets the dog outside to the safety of the backyard.
7:58:05	Gives toddler the newly found tiger.
7:58:18	Apologizes to middle schooler. Asks him how soccer is going. Manages to give him her full attention for forty seconds.
7:58:58	Sees toddler doing potty wiggle by the bathroom door.
7:58:59	Gets toddler to bathroom in time.

7:59:11	Assures teenage daughter that the black top and black miniskirt look even better than outfit number one.
7:59:14	Calls daughter chic and is rewarded with a smile and, "Thanks, Mom." Keeps the peace.
7:59:23	Wipes toddler's butt.
7:59:25	Kisses husband good-bye.
7:59:28	Tells husband he looks great. Really means it.
7:59:31	Gets toddler dressed.
7:59:56	Makes it back to the kitchen table while middle schooler is still sitting there.
7:59:57	Apologizes and resumes conversation about soccer. Tries not to wonder if the quiet in the next room is a good thing or not.

A Wonderful, Amazing, Stupendous, Inspiring, Butt-Kicking Real-Life Story

As a teenager, Judee sang in clubs and dreamed of the touring life. Somehow she ended up a single mom raising two girls. Times weren't always easy, and money was tight. When nine-year-old Julie asked for piano lessons, Judee had to say no. She never forgot the sadness on her daughter's face.

Years later, long after Judee and Julie became the owners of a thriving custom optical manufacturing business, they were wining and dining at a black-tie benefit just a few weeks before Julie's thirtieth birthday. As they browsed the items up for auction, Judee saw Julie eyeing a beautiful Schafer and Sons piano with the same wistful, pleading expression that had begged for lessons long ago. But now, Judee could do something about it.

Judee's hand was first in the air when bidding started on the piano, and she would not be deterred. This gift would fulfill Julie's long-held dream. Her daughter would have that piano! Unfettered by rules of decorum and a room full of bluebloods, Judee stood up and announced to her competitor, "You can bid as high as you want, but this is a present for my daughter's thirtieth birthday. She's going to have that piano and I'm not going to stop bidding until it's hers!"

That very piano now sits in Julie's living room, and she plays it beautifully and often. Though she's shy about playing in front of other people, she always makes an exception for her mom.

If Women Ran the World . . .
Women would know that whatever we can do in any given moment is enough. As a result, guilt, beating ourselves up, and the phrase "I should" would cease to exist.

A Butt-Kicking Inspiration

In the 1860s and 1870s, when Anna Jarvis was a little girl, she often heard her mother wish that there was a day commemorating all mothers for their wonderful deeds of service to their families. Years later, after her mother died in 1905, she vowed to fulfill her mother's wish.

The following year, Anna Jarvis gathered with friends on the first anniversary of her mother's death to honor and celebrate all the wonderful things her mother had done. By the second anniversary of her mother's death, she had convinced her mother's coworkers at the Andrews Church to form a Mother's Day Memorial Committee. Church leaders also passed a resolution favoring the founding of Mother's Day and held a memorial service for Anna's mother.

Anna Jarvis's efforts didn't stop there. She wrote to leaders in business and politics on all levels, and promoted her idea for a National Mother's Day every chance she had. By the third anniversary of her mother's death, she had garnered enough support that full programs were held at two Andrews Churches to honor *all* mothers.

Through Anna Jarvis's continued efforts, Mother's Day was observed in forty-five states, Puerto Rico, Canada, and Mexico in 1909 and the Governor of West Virginia issued the first Mother's Day proclamation in 1910. Then in 1914, just nine years after her mother's death, a joint resolution was passed by the United States House and Senate naming the second Sunday in May Mother's Day. At a time when women had not yet earned the right to vote, Anna Jarvis convinced leaders at the highest level to vote for a day that honors mothers everywhere. She fulfilled her mother's wish that all mothers are forever celebrated for the wonderful things they do.

Check out:
www.genealogy.about.com

The Wonderful, Amazing, Stupendous, Inspiring, Butt-Kicking Things I've Done for My Family

Have you ever had one of those days where you felt like nothing you did was enough? Even though you made it to your son's soccer game, cooked a tasty dinner that included everyone's favorite vegetable (all *five* of them), and went to three different stores in *three different zip codes* before finding the "must have" shoes of the century for your teenager, all you remember is that you were late to your daughter's ballet class, forgot that your son now hates broccoli, and learned from your teenager that the color shoes you bought are "so yesterday." All you can imagine is a breaking news headline flashing on your TV screen (next to an old yearbook picture you hoped to never see again): "Arrest this woman! She did not do enough today!"

When you're having a day like that, pull out your *Wonderful, Amazing, Stupendous, Inspiring, Butt-Kicking Things I've Done For My Family* list so you can remember all the fabulous things you *have* done instead of berating yourself for all the things you *should* have done. Applaud yourself for the time you surprised your partner with a fabulous just-because night out (or in). Take a bow for inviting all the kids in your son's grade at his new school to a party so they would think he was cool before the first day.

You are one amazing woman. You kick butt for your family every day. Let your list be the cure any time you catch a case of not enough-itis. Instead of imagining the Not Enough Police at your door, you'll see the *Get Sh*t Done Prize Patrol* instead.

You are one amazing woman.
You kick butt for your
family every day.

Butt-Kicking Things I've Done for My Family

_____

_____

_____

_____

_____

_____

_____

_____

_____

A Wonderful, Amazing, Stupendous, Inspiring, Butt-Kicking Real-Life Story

When my mom, Sally, went into labor with my brother, she thought she was prepared for anything. She'd had a standard, not-horribly-long first labor with my sister, and a dramatic, barely-made-it-to-the-hospital-and-out-of-the-elevator-before-nearly-giving-birth-in-the-hallway labor with me. Whatever baby number three had planned for her, she knew she could handle it.

She wasn't ready, however, to hear growing panic in the doctors' voices, or to have my dad whisked from the room with no explanation. She hadn't expected to deliver a son who'd need life-saving surgery the second day of his life. Nor had she expected the doctors to advise her against the procedure. "He'll ruin your lives. He'll ruin your daughters' lives. You can still have more children. You should let him die," they said. My mom, barely able to resist her urge to slap the doctor across the face (especially impressive considering all the postpregnancy hormones zooming through her body), said, "This is my child. He's living and breathing right now. I'm going to do whatever I can to give him the best life possible." For the past twenty-nine years, my mom has done exactly that. It's what women do, no matter what situation we're faced with.

If Women Ran the World . . .
Women would always trust and value
their own opinions, not just when
other people are obviously wrong,
inconsiderate, and stupid.

A Butt-Kicking Inspiration

When Annie Dodge Wauneka was eight years old, an influenza epidemic killed thousands of Navajos on the reservation where she lived. The mild case she contracted left her resistant to the disease, and she helped many people too sick to help themselves.

Through the years her commitment to helping others played a role in everything she did, eventually leading to her election to the Tribal Council in 1951 (she was only the second woman to achieve this feat). While she was in office, she worked to make life better for Navajo families by improving health care for pregnant mothers and babies and explaining the importance of tuberculosis vaccinations. Because of her efforts, many Navajos experienced life-saving medical practices and better living conditions.

Annie Dodge Wauneka received the Presidential Medal of Freedom in 1963 and was named "The Legendary Mother of the Navajo Nation" by the Navajo Council in 1984. Recently, a book was written that details all the ways she made life better for others. It is aptly titled, *I'll Go and Do More.*

Check out: *www.greatwomen.org*

The Three Ways I Kicked Butt Today

So it's 11:00 p.m. and you're curled up in bed, trying to quiet your mind after another jam-packed day. You really want to fall asleep, because in about six hours, some annoying song is going to start blaring from your alarm (probably with a tune so cheery it could turn even the nicest person into a crazed maniac).

Unfortunately, your mind is not cooperating with you. It can't stop wondering how you're going to finish sewing your ten-year-old's school play costume by 7:00 p.m. (which is when he needs to wear it) when you have one of those all-day meetings where your lunch hour isn't really your own, and you've promised your daughter you will help her find a new top for a date she actually asked your advice about. You decide to get up an hour earlier to finish sewing, and just as you are about to fall asleep you wonder if an hour will be enough time, or if you really should be attempting to use a needle (or anything sharp for that matter) that early in the morning. Wide awake once again, you try to decide if you should turn on the light and start sewing now. You also wish the mice and birds who fixed Cinderella's ball gown made house calls.

Here's a way to take back control of your mind. Instead of focusing on everything you have to do tomorrow, think about three ways you kicked butt today. Just twenty-four hours ago, you were lying in the same place wondering how you were going to manage it all, but like always, you managed just fine. Pat yourself on the back for everything you accomplished, and know that just like you kicked butt today, you'll wake up and kick butt tomorrow. You are one amazing woman, and you don't need to worry.

Women always get sh*t done.

The Three Ways I Kicked Butt Today

(1) _____

_____

_____

_____

_____

_____

_____

_____

_____

②

③

A Butt-Kicking Inspiration

Patricia Schroeder was first elected to Congress in 1972, and she served twelve consecutive terms as a Representative from Colorado before retiring from Congress in 1996. A mother of two young children at the time she was first elected, she was committed to making things better for all women, knowing that families would benefit as a result of her efforts. Among the many ways Patricia Schroeder kicked butt for families, she

❊ Wrote the Family and Medical Leave Act in 1985, which she finally saw passed into law in 1993;

❊ Introduced the Military Family Act, which was passed into law in 1985;

❊ Chaired the Select Committee on Children, Youth, and Families; and

❊ Co-chaired the Congressional Caucus on Women's Issues.

Patricia Schroeder was elected to the National Women's Hall of Fame in 1995 due in part to her "unblinking commitment to represent the interests of women and their families at the highest levels of government." Thanks to her efforts, life is easier for millions of civilian and military wives and moms living today.

Check out: *www.greatwomen.org*

If Women Ran the World, Here's What Might Get Done . . .

Every day, millions of women around the world are doing their best to care for their loved ones. While our situations and circumstances are different, the acts of caring come from the same beautiful place inside us women. If women ran the world, perhaps CNN would become the Caring News Network, a twenty-four-hour station dedicated to all the compassionate things women do for their families, for other people, and for the world.

I can think of enough stories to last my lifetime. Headlines like these would be typical daily occurrences:

✳ Kentucky Gal Pals Band Together to Aid Bed-Resting Moms-to-Be

✳ "Equal Rights Equal Pay" No Longer Just a Battle Cry

✳ *If Women Ran the World* Author Forms Foundation to Empower Women Worldwide

What stories can you envision
would be told if women really
ran the world?

What stories would you tell if
you were in charge?

What would you do if you
ran the world?

If I Ran the World, Here's What
I Would Get Done . . .

_____

_____

_____

_____

_____

_____

_____

Doing . . . for Our Friends

Women are the best cheerleaders for our friends. We do for our friends whenever, wherever, and however we can, whether it's to make the hard moments easier or the easy moments joyful.

When a friend needs to cry, we bring the tissues, offer our shoulder, listen to whatever she manages to say between the sobs, and hand her chocolate as she needs it.

When a friend needs to laugh, we rent the silliest comedies around, always have a story or two on stand-by, and hand her chocolate as she needs it.

When a friend needs to hit something (and we don't want her to get arrested), we take her to a kickboxing class, buy her the entire Tae Bo DVD series, and bring her a month's supply of chocolate so she'll have some handy whenever she needs it.

Women always know the right words or gestures to remind a friend that she is wonderful. We have championed and supported each other long before the words "You go girl" were ever strung together. Ask a woman from any place or point in history and I think she'd agree: There really is nothing like a girlfriend.

21 Things the Average Woman Does for Her Friends . . . (Often All in One Afternoon)

1. Listens as a friend vents about how her egotistical boss humiliated her.

2. Jokingly offers to sneak into boss's home, take pictures of him in the shower, and post them on the Internet.

3. Makes friend laugh.

4. Listens some more and assures friend her feelings are completely justified.

5. Sends friend e-card to cheer her up.

6. Calls a mutual friend to plan a surprise night of fun for friend with the boss from hell.

7. Listens as mutual friend shares the news of her promotion.

8. Sends mutual friend a congratulatory e-card.

9. Makes note to self to buy fun, you-are-amazing type presents for both friends before night of fun.

10. Mixes up some brownies for eight-months-pregnant neighbor, who mentioned she had a craving earlier in the day.

11. E-mails a job-hunting friend's résumé to entire contact list.

12. Mentions how wonderful, amazing, stupendous, inspiring, and butt-kicking job-hunting friend is in the e-mail.

13. Takes brownies over to neighbor, along with several DVDs that are free of any reference to stretch marks, swollen feet, or colicky babies.

14. Feeds neighbor's toddler, who is hungry now and doesn't care that Daddy will be home in ten minutes, so neighbor doesn't have to stand on her feet.

15. Makes daily phone call to a recently single friend, so she has at least one voicemail message to come home to.

16. When recently single friend (who is home from work early and all sobbed out) answers the phone, insists friend come over immediately for some movie and ice cream therapy.

17. Checks freezer and makes emergency trip to local market.

18. Buys three ice cream flavors for recently single friend to choose from.

19. Also grabs whipped cream, hot fudge, and every pack of peanut M&Ms (recently single friend's favorite) by the register.

20. While waiting for recently single friend, hides
     every magazine that makes mention of sex,
     romantic get-a-ways, or men in general.

21. Bans husband to upstairs den to create a safe,
     man-free, chicks-rule zone.

A Wonderful, Amazing, Stupendous, Inspiring, Butt-Kicking Real-Life Story

Alene married for the second time when she was twenty-eight, and she was determined to make marriage number two a success. She gave up everything for her second husband. Not just friends and relatives, but her identity, too. She believed *he* was who she was.

A second divorce wasn't part of the plan, but neither was having a husband who'd rather hold his secretary's hand than his wife's. When Alene shared the news with her neighbor Susan, Susan replied, "Oh goody. Now I'll have someone to play with."

Making Alene laugh was the first of many ways Susan supported her friend. For months, Alene spent almost every night at Susan's house, where Susan fed her, listened to her, handed her tissues, and told her she was fabulous. On the rare nights Alene wasn't at Susan's house, they talked on the phone for hours, watching television and doing needlepoint. Susan took Alene everywhere she went, not minding any necessary retreats to the bathroom to combat a sudden onslaught of tears. Spouse or no spouse, Susan showed Alene that she would never be alone. She also helped Alene realize that she would always be loved.

If Women Ran the World . . .
Happily ever after wouldn't
require a Y chromosome.

A Butt-Kicking Inspiration

Did you know that twenty-two million American women smoke? Did you know that most of them want to quit? Did you know that a woman who is supported by her friends and family when she is trying to quit is fifty percent more likely to quit successfully?

The American Legacy Foundation knew these facts and in 2002 they did something about them. They started the Circle of Friends campaign, a grassroots movement designed to create the kind of support networks women are especially gifted at creating. The campaign makes it possible for women to support their friends in many ways, including

※ Wearing the campaign's symbol of hope, the Sunburst, to honor a friend's attempt to quit.

※ Sending an e-card to encourage a friend trying to quit, reassure a friend who couldn't quit, or congratulate a friend who did quit.

※ Giving a Friendship Coupon offering to pamper a friend by taking her to lunch, treating her to a manicure, or in some way celebrating her for the great job she is doing.

Over 178,000 women die from tobacco-related diseases in the United States each year. By making it easier for women to help their friends quit smoking for good, perhaps the Circle of Friends will put an end to that statistic once and for all.

Check out: *www.join-the-circle.org*
to learn more about how
you can help your friends
quit smoking for good.

A Butt-Kicking What If . . .

Do you remember the movie *Thelma and Louise*? Do you remember how their fun, need-to-get-away-from-it-all road trip took on a whole new meaning after Louise shot a would-be rapist who was attacking Thelma? Do you remember their fear that the local police*men* would somehow blame Thelma for what nearly happened to her and arrest Louise for murder instead of understanding that she was defending her friend? Do you remember Thelma and Louise's choice at the end of the movie to drive over a cliff, saying no to the testosterone-driven society that said no to them?

What if their story never needed to be written? What if we lived in a world where women knew that the laws keeping them safe carried stiffer penalties (and were thus more important) than the laws for tax fraud? What if we lived in a world where there were *Charm Schools for Treating Women Right*, with classes like "Catcalls Are Never Okay" and "Don't Even Think about Using the B Word" required for everyone? What if we lived in a world where the phrase "crimes against women" never needed to be used again? What if the *Wonderful, Amazing, Stupendous, Inspiring, Butt-Kicking Friendship Awards* were an annual tradition, with more viewers than the Super Bowl?

We have the power to create this world today. Right now, we can band together with our girlfriends, put on our marching shoes, and create the butt-kicking, estrogen-celebrating, women-rock world every woman deserves.

What butt-kicking what ifs are you ready to march for?

What butt-kicking what ifs would you like to see?

Butt-Kicking What Ifs

_____

_____

_____

_____

_____

_____

_____

_____

_____

A Wonderful, Amazing, Stupendous, Inspiring, Butt-Kicking Real-Life Story

When Jennifer's fiancé left her one month before their wedding, she cried on the phone to her best friend, Dawn, for hours, asking all the normal questions someone in her position would ask. *Why did he leave? Is there someone else? Should I hire a hit man?*

Just when Jennifer thought she was calm enough to hang up the phone, she had a thought that made her cry even harder than before. Not only did the man of her dreams turn out to be a nightmare, but now there would be no wedding presents to open. There would be no matching glassware, let alone glasses with stems, from her registry. Instead, she was stuck with burnt spatulas, scratched Teflon, and three generations of mismatched, incomplete silverware . . . quite possibly for the rest of her life!

While Dawn didn't have the answers to Jennifer's initial questions (tempting as the hit man was), beautiful kitchenware was an issue she could do something about. Instead of returning the wedding present she'd bought for Jennifer, Dawn sent it to her as a housewarming present. Dawn also encouraged many of their friends to do the same. Soon, Jennifer's kitchen was filled with full, matching sets from her registry (she even had a few doubles to exchange) and some beautiful sunflower-themed extras from Dawn in honor of Jennifer's favorite flower.

When Jennifer thinks back to that time of her life, there's a lot she doesn't remember. But she does know she was grateful that her best friend was loyal to her when she most needed to be able to trust someone.

If Women Ran the World . . . There would be a Nobel Prize for Friendship.

A Butt-Kicking Inspiration

Iris Rainer Dart's cousin and close friend, Sandy, once said to her, "When one of us dies, I hope it's me first, because I couldn't stand to live in a world that didn't have you in it." Iris Rainer Dart decided to do something to honor the amazing beauty that exists in friendship among women. The novel *Beaches* was born as a result.

Beaches was published only after another of her novels (a scandalous tale about young men in Hollywood) was a great success. The wonderful story of two friends who meet on a beach as children and spend decades supporting, inspiring, and kicking butt for each other—a story publishers initially thought would lack commercial appeal—became a *New York Times* best seller and led to both a wildly popular movie and a sequel. Iris Rainer Dart once said, "I could only tell a story of how crucial my women friends are to my well-being, how their love has guided me through this life, how I don't think I could have made it without them."

By writing a story that celebrates the kind of friendships she has experienced, Iris Rainer Dart wrote a story that celebrates what is inspiring about friendship among all women.

Send a Friend a Do-O-Gram

I'll never forget the time I showed up at my friend Marcia's house after a job interview practically crawling to her door with a sprained back. As soon as she saw me, Marcia helped me to a chair; brought me a heating pad, an ice pack, a pillow, and a footrest; offered me an array of painkillers; asked if I wanted a cocktail instead; found me some comfy clothes to change into; helped me put them on without any sharp pain or need for cursing; insisted I stay the night in her guest room; and single-handedly gave new meaning to five-star treatment in about two minutes flat.

I'm sure all of us can think of a friend (or ten) who has cared for us like Marcia did for me, and would love to do something awesome and original to say thanks. Why not send that friend a Do-O-Gram? Honor, pamper, and celebrate her for honoring, pampering, and celebrating you. After all, she is one wonderful, amazing, stupendous, inspiring, butt-kicking friend. Go ahead and tell her so.

In recognition of the wonderful, amazing, stupendous, inspiring, butt-kicking friend you are, and for the time you

_____

_____

_____

I hereby present you with _____

_____

_____

_____

and a lifetime membership in the Get Sh*t Done Hall of Fame ※

※ MEMBERSHIP COMES WITH AN UNLIMITED SUPPLY OF LISTENING, SHOULDER LENDING, AND HUGS, AND A PERMANENT INVITATION TO ALL CHICKFLICK MARATHONS, GIRLS' NIGHT OUTS, AND ICE CREAM PALOOZAS.

In recognition of the wonderful, amazing, stupendous, inspiring, butt-kicking friend you are, and for the time you

_____

_____

_____

I hereby present you with _____

_____

_____

_____

and a lifetime membership in the Get Sh*t Done Hall of Fame ※

※ MEMBERSHIP COMES WITH AN UNLIMITED SUPPLY OF LISTENING, SHOULDER LENDING, AND HUGS, AND A PERMANENT INVITATION TO ALL CHICKFLICK MARATHONS, GIRLS' NIGHT OUTS, AND ICE CREAM PALOOZAS.

In recognition of the wonderful, amazing, stupendous, inspiring, butt-kicking friend you are, and for the time you

_____

_____

_____

I hereby present you with _____

_____

_____

_____

and a lifetime membership in the Get Sh*t Done Hall of Fame ✷

✷ MEMBERSHIP COMES WITH AN UNLIMITED SUPPLY OF LISTENING, SHOULDER LENDING, AND HUGS, AND A PERMANENT INVITATION TO ALL CHICKFLICK MARATHONS, GIRLS' NIGHT OUTS, AND ICE CREAM PALOOZAS.

In recognition of the wonderful, amazing, stupendous, inspiring, butt-kicking friend you are, and for the time you

_____

_____

_____

I hereby present you with _____

_____

_____

_____

and a lifetime membership in the Get Sh*t Done Hall of Fame ✳

✳ MEMBERSHIP COMES WITH AN UNLIMITED SUPPLY OF LISTENING, SHOULDER LENDING, AND HUGS, AND A PERMANENT INVITATION TO ALL CHICKFLICK MARATHONS, GIRLS' NIGHT OUTS, AND ICE CREAM PALOOZAS.

A Butt-Kicking Inspiration

When Sharon Henifin and Becky Olson met in 1991, they didn't know they would soon have something more in common than the company where they worked. Over the next few years, both became breast cancer survivors. Through their experiences, they realized that oftentimes friends who want to help don't always know what to do. They also realized there was something they could do so no woman would ever have to feel like she was fighting breast cancer alone.

Becky and Sharon started Breast Friends in August 2000. Their mission is "helping women survive the trauma of breast cancer, one friend at a time." More than 100,000 people have visited their Web site, which features a Friends and Family tab listing butt-kicking things women can do to help a friend with the disease. They have also created *First I Cry* packets for women diagnosed with the disease. These pink envelopes contain a message of hope, a silk screened handkerchief, and a sealed envelope to be given to a friend that contains tips for how the friend can help. Breast Friends has also created a Volunteer Match program for any woman who does not have a friend nearby to support her.

Breast Friends has received grants from the Susan G. Komen Foundation and won the Editor's Choice Award from *www.healingwell.com*. Most importantly, the organization has made it easier for women to do great things for friends in need.

Check out: *www.breastfriends.com*

A Wonderful, Amazing, Stupendous, Inspiring, Butt-Kicking Real-Life Story

Jyn and I were roommates for four years, until she got married and I moved to California, ending what we joked was the longest relationship for both of us. Jyn accepted me just as I am, even the anal, overly detailed side that created a checklist to help her get out of the apartment in one trip (and she forgave me for including things like "Make sure oven and stove are off," which she later admitted were necessary).

When Jyn came to visit me the following summer, my California experience was a far cry from Disneyland. My job contract had just been terminated, my relationship was failing, and I was living 3,000 miles from all the people I wanted to smear my mascara in front of the most. Needless to say, Jyn's shoulder worked overtime that trip.

I think it took Jyn's shoulder hours to dry the day she left. That afternoon, I found her "Raving Fans" notebook. Ever since I've known Jyn, she's had a Raving Fans notebook, keeping every card and note where someone has complimented her (a handy tool as she's traversed the road of rejection an actor often faces). As I picked up the notebook, my first thought was, "I knew she wouldn't be able to survive without my checklists on the door!" Then, I opened it and read the following: A start to your "Raving Fans," Kudos, Feeling-down-need-to-remember-how-fabulous-

I-am-book! For my incredibly talented, intelligent, creative, ambitious, beautiful friend.

I realized Jyn created a Raving Fans notebook for me. She knew exactly what I needed. Our friends always do.

If Women Ran the World . . .
We would each have a large Raving
Fans club, complete with a website,
fan mail, and weekly chats that
celebrate our greatness.

If Women Ran the World, Here's What Might Get Done . . .

I'm sure all of us can think of times in our lives when, if it wasn't for our girlfriends, our sense of humor (not to mention our sanity) would not be intact today. Certainly, part of life, liberty, and the pursuit of happiness for women involves the freedom to call our girlfriends and scream (be it in anger, excitement, or utter disbelief), "You are *not* going to believe what happened today!"

It's hard to believe that, in this day and age, not all women are free to call or see their girlfriends, let alone talk freely when they are given the chance to be with other women. If women ran the world, no husband, father, brother, or government law or agency would ever have power, permission, or the legal right to control what a woman thinks or her freedom to share her thoughts with other women. Chocolate and ice cream therapy time with girlfriends would be an inalienable right listed in every constitution, and a practice celebrated often. Anyone who felt threatened by these freedoms would have no legal authority or agency to back them up, and would be told to, quite simply, "Get over it." Years of therapy would also be suggested. Meanwhile, women around the world would continue to do what many of us do now, kick butt for our friends each and every day.

What other butt-kicking things do you think would happen if women ran the world?

How would you kick butt if you ran the world?

If I Ran the World, Here's What I Would Get Done . . .

_____

_____

_____

_____

_____

_____

_____

_____

Doing . . . for Our Jobs

Women have kicked butt in the working world long before we were welcomed into the corporate realm of nine to five. Women have served in armies and toiled in fields, earning just as many sunburns and blistered hands as the men alongside them. For centuries, women have wielded scalpels, understood the language of Einstein and Newton, and written as beautifully as Shakespeare. We have invented, influenced, and discovered even as we've had to flee our countries, publish our words under male names, see our reputations destroyed, face the threat of lockup (be it in jail or a sanitarium), or even lose our lives in the process.

Women kick butt because we see past the bottom line *and* we speak up and speak out for causes or colleagues when no one else will. Women kick butt because we challenge outdated policies that no longer work (and because we notice they aren't working in the first place). Women kick butt because we, as Margaret Thatcher said, "stick to a job and get on with it when everyone else walks off and leaves." Today and always, working women get sh*t done.

10 Butt-Kicking Things Women Do at Work . . . (That *Aren't* in Our Job Descriptions)

1. Spends lunch hour listening to a colleague's career-breaking presentation (for the third day in a row).

2. Cleans up other people's messes (the no-broom-required type).

3. Covers for a colleague who's either on the phone with a huffy teenager, in the bathroom fixing meltdown-smeared mascara, or on a desperate, panicked search for a vending machine with peanut M&Ms.

4. Removes ketchup stain from a colleague's shirt in under thirty seconds, saving colleague from horrible embarrassment in front of company's biggest clients (and from earning the nickname "ketchup boy").

5. Figures out former colleague's password, gaining access to file everyone needs, by remembering the nickname of former colleague's second (of six) pet poodles and the year that poodle won third place in town Doggy Parade.

6. Buys cards for all her coworkers' birthdays, makes sure everyone signs them, and organizes lunch celebrations.

7. Wipes off countertop in the office kitchen because she can't stand a messy kitchen anywhere.

8. Always contributes something yummy to the snack table.

9. Keeps a drawer filled with tampons, mouthwash, needle and thread, hairspray, nail files, antacid, and Motrin for anyone in the midst of a crisis.

10. Listens to raving colleagues, clients, or managers and helps them feel better (even if she never says a word).

A Wonderful, Amazing, Stupendous, Inspiring, Butt-Kicking Real-Life Story

A former flower child and follower of the Grateful Dead, Marcia lived an early life that was full of adventure, and that continued as she worked her way up the corporate ladder and became an editor for the *New York Times* regional newspapers. Within a twenty-four-hour time span, Marcia would race to meet a deadline at her office in Florida and then jet to the West Coast or even Europe for a conference or event she needed to cover. Marcia has had tea in the White House with Barbara Bush, lunch at the Plaza with Martha Stewart, and dinner at the Smithsonian's Air and Space Museum with Ben Bradlee and Art Buchwald. Though she assures me otherwise, it wouldn't have surprised me if these three exploits occurred in the same day!

No matter how close she was to a deadline or whatever foreign city she was in for the day, Marcia always took the time to stand up for her colleagues. One time Marcia convinced senior editors at her newspaper to give a reporter colleague, exhausted from just finishing a difficult series on death and dying, a spa gift certificate. Marcia knew that something more than the typical dinner gift certificate was exactly what her colleague needed after researching the depressing stats on hospice care and living wills. Despite her own assignments, despite her busy travel schedule, despite her work as president of the American Association of Sunday and Features Editors, Marcia made sure her colleague received the thanks she deserved. Marcia was also the only one who thought to do so.

Marcia thinks she's helped her colleagues in "small ways," but actually, her impact has been significant. Marcia not only recognizes her colleagues' worth, she also insists that other people do the same.

If Women Ran the World . . .
Great praise and even greater raises would be earned for seeing *more than* the corporate bottom line.

A Butt-Kicking Inspiration

Mary McLeod Bethune was born in 1875 to two former slaves. The fifteenth of seventeen children, she was one of the few children in her family not born into slavery herself. She had a love of learning and thrived at the one-room school near her home, eventually earning scholarships to both Scotia Seminary and Dwight Moody's Institute for Home and Foreign Missions.

Wanting to help educate other African American women and provide opportunities for them, she started the Daytona Literary and Industrial School for Training Negro Girls in 1904. Whether she was convincing leading philanthropists of the day to contribute or serving on advisory Boards under both President Herbert Hoover and President Franklin Delano Roosevelt, she did what was necessary for her school and her students to thrive.

Mary McLeod Bethune worked hard because she wanted everyone to have access to education and job opportunities. Through her efforts, her school (started with just $1.50 and five students) evolved into Bethune Cookman College, a four-year college that thousands have graduated from. Because of Mary McLeod Bethune, women of many races have gained access to the workplace, and achieved great successes in a variety of fields, including medicine, business, and government. Because of Mary McLeod Bethune, more women have had a chance to do great things.

Check out: *www.cookman.edu*

The Wonderful, Amazing, Stupendous, Inspiring, Butt-Kicking Things Women Did First

Did you know that a woman was the first to

❉ Win the Nobel Prize twice? (Marie Curie, 1903 in Physics and 1911 in Chemistry)

❉ Win an Oscar and a Tony in the same year? (Ellen Burstyn in 1975 for the movie *Alice Doesn't Live Here Anymore* and the play *Same Time, Next Year*)

❉ Go over Niagara Falls in a barrel? (Annie Edson Taylor in 1901)

Did you know that a woman invented AZT (the major AIDS-fighting drug), Kevlar (the main ingredient in bulletproof vests), the vaccination for smallpox, and one of my personal favorites, the drip coffeemaker?

What wonderful, amazing, stupendous, inspiring, butt-kicking ideas have you thought of?

What wonderful, amazing, stupendous, inspiring, butt-kicking things do you want to do first?

You *are* a woman. You *are* inherently good enough, smart enough, and talented enough. Go ahead and make your *Butt-Kicking Things I Plan to Do First List* today. Start developing, discovering, and inventing your ideas now. Let your name be a wonderful addition to the *World's Butt-Kicking Famous First Women List*.

Butt-Kicking Things I Plan to Do First

_____

_____

_____

_____

_____

_____

_____

_____

_____

A Butt-Kicking Inspiration

When Juliette Gordon Low met Boy Scouts founder Sir Robert Baden-Powell in 1911 while she was living in England, she realized what she wanted to do with the rest of her life. Just a few months after that fateful day, she returned to the United States and called a girlfriend, saying, "I've got something for the girls of Savannah, and all of America, and all the world, and we're going to start it tonight!"

Since Juliette Low formed the first troop of eighteen girls on March 12, 1912, the Girl Scouts has become an international organization with 3.6 million members throughout the United States and in more than 80 countries worldwide. It was also one of the first organizations to include disabled girls among its ranks, and it has been working to inform and educate key leaders of Congress through its Public Policy and Advocacy office, formed in 1952. Juliette Low was a pioneer in encouraging *all* girls to believe in and prepare for professional success outside the home. In fact, of all the women who have been elected to Congress, two-thirds have been Girl Scouts!

Juliette Gordon Low spent years in the early twentieth century searching for something "useful" to do with her life. By founding Girl Scouts, she has inspired millions of girls to do something amazing with their lives.

Check out: *www.girlscouts.org*

A Wonderful, Amazing, Stupendous, Inspiring, Butt-Kicking Real-Life Story

Judy discovered her love of design during her second marriage, to Tom, a successful architect in the Atlanta area. The precision and calculation involved in design work mesmerized Judy's inner math whiz, and she begged Tom to give her a chance. He eventually agreed, and Judy's very first house design was featured in a front-page article in the Home section of the Atlanta *Journal-Constitution* Sunday paper.

While Tom believed in Judy at first, it became harder for him to accept that his wife's success was surpassing his own, despite his education and years of experience. Tom's mother spent months begging Judy to stop competing with her son, to be the wife and mom she "was meant to be." Judy's dad, after seeing Judy's picture in yet another magazine, told her she looked tired and suggested that perhaps her work was too stressful for a woman.

Judy disagreed, and she refused to follow the path others had laid out for her. She continued her design work, eventually becoming a builder and starting her own business, Handcrafted Homes, Inc., because she knew she could do a better job constructing her designs than any builder she could hire. Despite the hooting and catcalls from construction workers who did not know she was the boss, despite the many male egos who couldn't believe a woman could know just as much if not more than them, Judy never accepted "I can't," "I won't," or "I don't know how" as part of her vocabulary. Judy has never once doubted her right to muddy her Cole Haan boots or don her pink suede toolbelt on any of her construction sites. Never once has she doubted her ability to succeed or pretended to be anything other than the fabulous woman she is.

If Women Ran the World . . .
The "old boys club" would exist only in history books. There would also be a lot more *her*story books available.

A Butt-Kicking Inspiration

When Felice Schwartz was born in 1925, women were lucky if they gained access to the workplace, much less received equal pay for equal work. For those women who were admitted to the land of nine to five, few options existed for them if they also wanted to have a family. Part-time work, job sharing, and flexible schedules had no place in the mainstream jargon of the early twentieth century.

Felice Schwartz decided to do something about this. In 1962, she formed the organization Catalyst to help women enter the workforce. From her kitchen table in suburban Ohio, her books *Making the Most of Your First Job* and *How to Go to Work When Your Husband Is Against It* inspired many. As the organization grew it shifted its focus to working directly with corporations and businesses to advance women, recognizing that change needed to occur *within* companies before change could occur for the women working there.

Today Catalyst is a leading non-profit research and advisory organization committed to achieving "a world that supports and encourages every woman in her career aspirations and places no limits on where her skills and energy can take her." Now with offices in New York, San Jose, and Toronto, Catalyst's history, mission, and vision is a wonderful example of what one woman can accomplish for herself. . . *and* for others.

Check out: *www.catalystwomen.org*

A Butt-Kicking What If . . .

Have you ever thought about all the wonderful ways women are allowed to kick butt today, ways that weren't available to our grandmothers and perhaps even our mothers? Isn't it amazing that

✳ Young girls can reach for a box of cereal and see a female athlete pictured on the front.

✳ Females of all ages now make up the majority of college undergraduates.

✳ Women not only head companies, we head countries.

Wouldn't it be even more amazing if

✳ Female athletic programs really did receive the time, money, and attention they were legally entitled to.

✳ Females of all races counted for at least half of all college professors.

✳ A woman was President of the United States.

What other butt-kicking things would you like to see in your lifetime?

How about in your daughter's or granddaughter's lifetime?

What butt-kicking what ifs can you imagine?

Butt-Kicking What Ifs

_____

_____

_____

_____

_____

_____

_____

_____

_____

If Women Ran the World,
Here's What Might Get Done . . .

Have you ever been talked down to, told no, or denied an opportunity because someone was intimidated by your fabulous femaleness? Have you ever felt like your ideas were pooh-poohed, ignored, or perhaps even laughed at because your name ends in an *a*, your power suit comes accessorized with pumps, and you use the lavatory with the dress symbol on it? Have you ever wanted to climb the highest mountain, link hands with women everywhere, and echo the words of former Congresswoman Pat Schroeder, "I have a brain and a uterus, and I use both," perhaps even adding the words "Deal with it" to the end?

If women ran the world, then no woman would ever be turned down, or talked down to, because of her gender. We wouldn't have to defend our theories, policies, or ideas any more or any less than our male counterparts. Our right to do what we want and our ability to get sh*t done would be unquestioned, unchallenged, and always assured. We would see

* Superstars in the WNBA earning as much as players in the NBA.

* Equal opportunity employment actually meaning an equal shot at *all* opportunities.

* Centuries where more women than men have served as President.

Imagine if women from every place and point in history had lived in a world like this. Imagine what the world would look like today. When women really do live in a world like this, imagine the amazing world we will create.

What amazing things would you do?

What kind of amazing world would you create if you were in charge?

If I Ran the World, Here's What I Would Get Done

_____

_____

_____

_____

_____

_____

_____

_____

_____

Doing . . . for the World

Women have always worked to make the world a better place (even though we've rarely been the ones with the power and authority to mess it up to start with). Whether we lived during the days when horse and buggy was our fastest means of travel, or today when we can go anywhere (even if we never leave our homes), women have

- Founded organizations, funded charities, and freed people no matter the laws, policies, or protestors that stood in our way.

- Marched on Washington (and across the country first if necessary) to make our voices heard.

- Wielded a pen and sometimes a sword for a cause or Constitution we believed in.

When women see something we can do for the world (be it locally, nationally, or internationally), we don't waste time seeking permission from some committee whose members are barely speaking to each other, or talking about how fabulous we are beforehand. Women don't hesitate to grab whatever or whoever is handy, go out into the world, and stand up for our beliefs, even if we are laughed at, spit on, or sprayed with tear gas for our efforts. Instead, we take care of business and we get sh*t done. We also manage to make the world a brighter and more peaceful place in the process.

12 Things Women Do for the World . . . (Even If No One Notices)

1. Teaches her children about giving by having them donate three of their toys to another child (eventually without tantrums, crossed arms, or stomping feet).

2. Makes volunteering at a soup kitchen at 6:00 a.m. Thanksgiving morning an annual family tradition.

3. Creates color-coded recycle bins that everyone in the house (including the dog) can understand.

4. Starts recycling program at work that even upper management can follow.

5. Uses lunch hour to draft a butt-kicking, no-one-can-resist-me donor letter for charity in need of funds.

6. Becomes self-appointed turn-off-those-extra-lights police (complete with whistle and ticket pad) both at home and at work.

7. Stays up half the night perfecting flyers for a community meeting, and then wakes up an hour early to hang them.

8. Bakes, races, runs, or walks for hours, days, or entire weekends for any cause or cure that will better the world.

9. Makes room in closet for new Donna Karan suit by donating clothes to a charity that helps other women dress for success.

10. Sends kind words along with sponsor check to a needy child halfway around the world.

11. Willingly sacrifices all ten new acrylic nails while building a home for Habitat for Humanity.

12. Realizes women around the world are mothers, sisters, friends, and daughters who share more similarities than differences.

A Wonderful, Amazing, Stupendous, Inspiring, Butt-Kicking Real-Life Story

Julie has always believed in the importance of conservation, long before green bins began dotting our curbsides on trash day. As a child she spent summers on the American River, and since her family's makeshift cabin was reached by helicopter, there was little room for carry-on bags (much less baggage to check). Julie knew the few things she was allowed to take with her had to last the entire summer. She learned that everything was valuable.

As an adult this lesson has guided many of her choices, from her commitment to recycling after trudging through trash in India that had been exported there by the United States, to her subscription to *UTNE Reader* magazine so she could learn more ways to conserve. Most recently, Julie decided she no longer wanted to start her day inhaling (and adding to) the smog on the freeway. She decided it was time to stop paying for a toll road that threatened wildlife and fauna near her home. She realized there was something else she could do.

Julie began riding her bicycle to a local train station so she could take the train to work, gaining time for herself on the train, a great new way to work out, and the satisfaction of knowing she was conserving resources in the process. Soon many of her colleagues expressed interest in doing the same. As a result, Julie started a Train/Bike to Work program at her company, paying for monthly train passes for anyone interested in trying this time-, resource-, and energy-saving commute. The program has become so popular that many of the participants' friends and family members have begun taking the train to their own jobs. Because of Julie, many people have realized there's something they can do for the world.

Julie doesn't consider herself an activist. She just wants to find, as she says, small ways to make a difference. The wonderful thing is oftentimes, like in Julie's case, the *small* ways make a *big* difference.

If Women Ran the World . . . The world, and everything and everyone in it, would be seen as valuable.

A Butt-Kicking Inspiration

Protecting the environment is a cause that's important to many people, and it's one that Marjory Stoneman Douglas championed throughout her 108-year life. During the first half of the twentieth century, she wielded her pen to protest the destruction of the Florida Everglades in both columns for the *Miami Herald* and a book entitled *The Everglades: River of Grass*. She understood early on that, besides being an important ecosystem for many plants and animals, the Everglades is the only source of drinking water for millions of residents living in Southern Florida. She also knew the area was being drained at an alarming rate.

In 1969, Marjory Stoneman Douglas formed Friends of the Everglades and took her place in front of bulldozers to prevent the building of a jetport that would further damage the area. The jetport was never built. For the last four decades, Friends of the Everglades has educated the public, legally challenged activities that threaten the area, and monitored all government policies that could impact the area. The organization now has 6,000 members and its entire Executive Team and Board of Directors are filled with volunteers.

Check out: *www.everglades.org*

Marjory Stoneman Douglas once said "find out what needs to be done and do it." The Friends of the Everglades continues to do just that.

A Butt-Kicking What If . . .

In 1950, Mother Teresa started the Missionaries of Charity and for more than forty years she traveled the world, never once ignoring or denying someone in need of help because of where they lived, what they looked like, or what they believed. She fed people, loved people, and cured people. She brought them hope when no one or nothing else could or tried.

What do you think the world would look like if Mother Teresa, along with starting her mission in 1950, had been appointed ruler of the world? How would the past fifty-some years have been different for us women? I think Mother Teresa would have made sure that

❋   Women everywhere always had enough
    food for their children.

❋   No mother would ever have to see her
    child go off to war.

❋   Leaders would be booted from office for
    spending more money on bombs than
    food and health care for their citizens.

❋   Women everywhere would know that their
    career options were utterly, absolutely, and
    completed unlimited.

What other policies do you think we would have seen if Mother Teresa were in charge?

What kind of world would she have created?

What butt-kicking what ifs do you think would be a reality today?

A Butt-Kicking Inspiration

Eradicating poverty is something many political leaders *talk* about. Mildred Robbins Leet has *done* something about it.

With her husband, Glen, she created Trickle Up in 1979, a program that provides capital and training directly to the world's most impoverished people so they don't have to wait for funds to trickle *through* protocol or red tape. Through the years, Trickle Up has made a special effort to help those often denied aid by other organizations, including single mothers, youth at risk, and refugees. The organization believes that *all* people have both the talent and the desire to escape from poverty.

Since the Leet's first used their own money to help start ten businesses by giving ten one hundred dollar grants to residents of Dominica, more than 135,000 businesses have been started or expanded in over 120 countries. Over 500,000 people in communities around the world have benefited as a result of Trickle Up's commitment to end poverty. For the last three decades, Trickle Up's actions have certainly spoken louder than many people's words.

Check out: *www.trickleup.org*

A Wonderful, Amazing, Stupendous, Inspiring, Butt-Kicking Real-Life Story

Ever since Jan can remember, she has had a special knack for helping people when they need it most. As a toddler, when her father was missing behind enemy lines in Korea, Jan would always know when she needed to pat her mom's leg and say, "It's going to be okay, Mommy. I'll take care of you." Giving people faith . . . in themselves, in others, and in the world . . . is Jan's way of doing for the world.

When she was a young mom, Jan spent time mentoring high school students, helping them see that a failed class or broken heart didn't mean the world was over (even if it felt like it at the time). As her children grew older, and after years of lending her ear to countless friends, family members, and colleagues, Jan decided to apply to graduate school and become a professional counselor. She knew that helping people who had lost their hope, and maybe even their will to live, was something she had to do. The University of San Diego admitted Jan to their Marriage and Family Therapy master's degree program, and two years later Jan graduated cum laude. She's been a professional counselor for nearly a decade.

Jan has made it her mission to help battered women and abused children believe in themselves, believe that they have something special to contribute to the world. She helps her clients realize that whatever bad situation happened was done *to* them and does not define who they *are*. Many of her clients have learned to live with joy, instead of in fear, for the first time in their lives. Because of Jan, countless women and children are no longer living as victims, but as victors. Because of Jan, the world has more women who know they are capable of doing great things.

If Women Ran the World . . .
Our daughters (and sons) would hear tales of women saving the world instead of women needing to be saved.

A Butt-Kicking Inspiration

When Joan Ganz Cooney created *Sesame Street* in 1969, she hoped the program would positively impact children's education. In particular, she wanted to help low-income children learn important fundamentals *before* they started school. Over the last four decades, *Sesame Street* has not only taught millions of children about letters, numbers, and languages, it has also been a showcase for diversity and acceptance. Through the years, *Sesame Street* has

* Cast a deaf actress to play a deaf character who is accepted by others in the neighborhood.

* Introduced an HIV-positive, five-year-old Muppet in the South African version as a result of the growing AIDS epidemic in that region.

* Created a segment called Global Grover in which Grover introduces children from around the world to each other to foster greater understanding.

* Seen the merger of its Israeli and Palestinian spin-offs to promote peace and acceptance among those cultures.

The words "Sunny days, sweepin' the clouds away" along with the show's messages of tolerance, acceptance, and understanding are now heard in over 140 countries around the world. Wouldn't it be amazing if what started with Joan Ganz Cooney's desire to help all children learn results in a worldwide generation that learns to love one another?

Check out:

www.tv.com/sesamestreet/show/887/ summary.html?q=sesame+street

The Wonderful, Amazing, Stupendous, Inspiring, Butt-Kicking Organizations Women Created

Did you know that the American Red Cross was founded by a woman (Clara Barton)? Did you know that the Salvation Army was co-founded by a woman (Catherine Booth)? Did you know that a woman (Eleanor Roosevelt) drafted the Declaration of Human Rights (passed by the United Nations on December 10, 1948) and was instrumental in helping the United Nations start UNICEF? Think of the billions of people around the world who have been helped by these three organizations, organizations that began due to the heart, mind, and guts of three amazing women.

And what about Mothers Against Drunk Driving (MADD)? Did you know that since MADD was founded by Candy Lightner in 1980, the legal drinking age was raised to twenty-one, all fifty states have lowered the blood alcohol concentration illegal drunk driving limit to .08, and that alcohol-related traffic fatalities have decreased 43 percent. In MADD's twenty-six-year history, 300,000 lives have been saved because of efforts that began with one woman!

Think about the Susan G. Komen Breast Cancer Foundation, which was founded on a promise made between two sisters, Susan Goodman Komen (who died of breast cancer in 1980) and Nancy Goodman Brinker (who promised her sister she would do everything possible to end breast cancer). Did you know that since Nancy Brinker founded the Komen Foundation in 1982 with just $200 and a shoebox of friends' names, the Foundation and its affiliates have raised more than $750 million, created a Web site that has educated millions, and started a toll-free hotline that helps thousands every year? In just over twenty years, the Komen foundation—through its pink ribbon campaign, its Races for the Cure, the Breast Cancer Research Stamp (the first postal stamp ever offered to generate funding for disease awareness and research), and its continued lobbying for better funding and legislation—has made sure that breast cancer has gone from a disease not discussed to a disease that many have survived and many more may never contract. As their Web site says, "a single person's vision can make a difference in the lives of millions."

And what about Oprah's Angel Network? What began as an invitation by Oprah in 1997 to her viewers to collect spare change for The Boys & Girls Clubs of America scholarships and to volunteer time building homes with

Habitat for Humanity is now a public charity that has raised more than $27 million dollars for charities and non-profit organizations that make a difference in people's lives around the world. Oprah's vision "to inspire individuals to create opportunities that help underserved people rise to their own potential" has enabled so many people to make an even bigger difference in the world.

What women do you admire for going into the world and making it a better place?

Who do you think of when you're searching for inspiration?

Who would you include on your list of Butt-Kicking Women Who Have Made a Difference?

Check out:
www.madd.org
www.oprah.com
www.komen.org

Butt-Kicking Women Who Have Made a Difference

_____

_____

_____

_____

_____

_____

_____

_____

_____

The Butt-Kicking Ways *I* Want to Make a Difference

What kind of difference do *you* want to make in the world? What special ways do you want to contribute? What brilliant ideas do you want to see next to your name in the *her*story books? Whether you have

❋   thought of a way to rid the world
      of heart disease, cancer, or the
      common cold;

❋   developed a theory that you know will
      end road rage, and could quite possibly
      lead to world peace; or,

❋   realized why the last five pounds
      people want to lose so often taunts
      and torments them instead of easily
      going away,

you *can* make the kind of difference you want to make, just like every woman you listed on your *Butt-Kicking Women Who Have Made a Difference* List. You are as smart, talented, and powerful as every woman you admire, so write down your wonderful, amazing, stupendous, inspiring, butt-kicking ideas today, right here and now. Give yourself permission to make the kind of difference *you* want to make, and like the butt-kicking woman you are, go out into the world and get sh*t done. Then add your own name to your *Butt-Kicking Women Who Have Made a Difference* List.

Butt-Kicking Ways I Want to
Make a Difference

If Women Ran the World, Here's What Might Get Done . . .

Throughout history, women have done amazing things for the world. We have saved lives and we have lengthened lives (be they people's, animals', or trees') even when our own lives were threatened (and sometimes lost) in the process. Unfortunately, many of the contributions women made to the world were unrecorded (or recorded but attributed to men). It's a sad fact, but we may never know all the wonderful, amazing, stupendous, inspiring, butt-kicking ways women gave to the world.

If women ran the world, the twenty-first century (and every century hereafter) would be the century of *her*-story. *Her*storians would record all the amazing ways women do for the world, and they would also make every effort to go back and correct every wrongly attributed contribution in history books from centuries past. No woman would ever again have her name smeared or her reputation destroyed for being brave enough to challenge a company that's using dangerous chemicals, endangering wildlife, or somehow profiting at the expense of others. No woman would ever again be accused of suffering from severe emotional distress, daddy issues, or PMS for challenging an unfair or just plain stupid government policy because there wouldn't be a testosterone-driven bureaucracy to feel threatened by her. Women everywhere would be free to do what needs to be done to better the world. We would also be thanked, instead of ignored, maligned, or attacked, for our efforts.

What would you like to be thanked for?

What would you do if you ran the world?

If I Ran the World, Here's What I
Would Get Done . . .

_____

_____

_____

_____

_____

_____

_____

_____

_____

Doing . . . for Ourselves

Women are amazing at getting sh*t done for their families, friends, jobs, and the world. Have you ever wondered why doing for ourselves oftentimes either:

- Comes after all the other doing we take on, or
- Makes us feel as guilty as that huge batch of cookies we ate all by ourselves?

Whatever reasons cross your mind and however much Incredible Hulk-like rage they may trigger, I say we not so politely expel these reasons from planet Earth. I say the next time you're wondering if you should pursue the job of your dreams, or if you really need that manicure you've been looking forward to all week, make your answer a resounding yes! Know that you deserve to get as much sh*t done for yourself as you chose to get done for all the other people, places, and things in your life.

Think of the day when women everywhere can choose where they want to live, what they want to do, and whose underwear they'll see crumpled by the shower in the morning. Grant yourself permission to enjoy and embrace every chance you have to kick butt for yourself. You deserve it. You are worth it. Women everywhere are worth it.

10 Things Women Intend to Do for Themselves . . .(and the 10 Things That Happen Instead)

1. Spend an hour soaking in a luxurious bubble bath. (Spend two hours drying the bathroom after giving toddler a bath.)

2. Stay up all night watching a marathon of all your favorite movies. (Fall asleep five minutes into a movie that only those with Y chromosomes find funny.)

3. Salt the popcorn with that special mix of sea salt and extra oil that only you seem to love. (Mix up several different batches seasoned exactly to everyone's preferences.)

4. Spend Saturday afternoon curled up by the fire reading some cheesy romance book and daydreaming about all sorts of possibilities. (Spend Sunday recovering from the cold you caught while running errands for everyone else during the rain on Saturday.)

5. Get a weekly manicure and pedicure. (Get weekly migraines.)

6.   Hire a cleaning service to help around the house. (Feel the need to have the house in somewhat respectable order before the cleaners are allowed inside.)

7.   Leave work at 6:00 p.m. every night to have more time to exercise, go out with friends, hang out with your family, or just sit on the couch and veg. (Let those last-minute, I-must-stay-and-finish-this-or-the-world-will-end-right-now tasks dictate your schedule on a regular basis.)

8.   Take a so-I-know-I'm-a-klutz-but-what-I-really-want-to-do-is-dance class. (Miss more classes than you actually attend because of the latest obligation that comes your way.)

9.   Volunteer for a cause that's meaningful to you. (Sacrifice precious sleep time to fulfill the commitment.)

10. Pursue your dreams. (Let your obligations to others take precedence over your obligation to yourself.)

A Wonderful, Amazing, Stupendous, Inspiring, Butt-Kicking Real-Life Story

As the eldest of five children and the only girl, Hilary felt like a mom to her brothers for most of her early life. Becoming one for real at age nineteen was *not* a part of her plan. Hilary and her boyfriend decided adoption was the best choice for them, but they changed their minds after Therese was born. They wanted to see if they really could have the happily-ever-after they'd dreamed about.

It didn't take long for Hilary to realize that she was not living her happily-ever-after dream-come-true. Often, Hilary felt like a single parent with two children instead of half of a couple raising one. For as long as she could remember, Hilary had put other people's needs before her own. She didn't want to live the rest of her life that way, too.

Determined to get her dreams back on track, Hilary returned to school. Even though her schedule was hectic and exhausting, even though she had to work three jobs (and occasionally worry she'd earn too much money for food stamps), even though she wished her occasional dozing in class was the result of a great frat party the night before instead of a night up with a sleepless child, Hilary was grateful to be moving toward her dreams once again. What kept her going was a promise she made to herself. She swore she would always give herself permission to pursue the life she really wanted. She swore she would never settle for anything less than the life of her dreams. Today, Hilary is a successful personal trainer and the proud mom of thirteen-year-old Therese. She is also thoroughly enjoying letting her dream life unfold.

If Women Ran the World . . . Doing for ourselves would be as guilt free as any nonfat, noncarb, non-tasting dessert is now.

A Butt-Kicking Inspiration

Shirley Ann Jackson has always loved math and science. As a child in the 1950s, she captured bees in jars and studied their behavior. She also put the Law of Motion to good use, winning many neighborhood go-cart races by positioning herself at the steepest part of the hill. Her love of math and science evolved into a passion for physics . . . the career she was born to have.

She won a full scholarship to MIT (she was one of only two African American women in her year) and she excelled in her classes, not letting anyone's opinion about her race or her gender keep her from the life of her dreams. She became the first black woman to earn a Ph.D. from MIT, completed years of important work involving semiconductors (CDs have never sounded better because of her), served as chairman of the Nuclear Regulatory Committee in the 1990s, and is currently the president of Rensselaer Polytechnic Institute.

Shirley Ann Jackson is one of ten butt-kicking women in science featured on the I was Wondering Web site which was created to show girls interested in science that they, too, can accomplish great things.

Check out: *www.iwaswondering.org*

Shirley Ann Jackson's advice to budding scientists
is a great reminder for all of us:

"Treasure your curiosity and nurture
your imagination. Have confidence
in yourself. Do not let others put
limits on you. Dare to imagine
the unimaginable."

The Wonderful, Amazing, Stupendous, Inspiring, Butt-Kicking Things I Demand From Now On

Have you ever had a day that went something like this:

* In the morning, you are told off by your teenager for, well, you're not sure why exactly, but you think it might have been for breathing.

* In the afternoon, you are told off by your boss for losing a client that wasn't even your responsibility to begin with.

* In the evening, you are told off by a cop for running a red light that you *know* was yellow.

Have you ever gotten to the end of a day like this and (besides craving a long bubble bath, a cocktail, or a ton of ice cream) wanted to grab the largest megaphone, climb the highest mountain, and loudly announce to the world that from this day forward, you deserve and demand better treatment than this?

What kind of days do you want to experience?

What wonderful ways do you want to be treated?

Whether you want five minutes to yourself when you first wake up or an equal chance at signing the biggest clients at work, write down every butt-kicking thing you are ready to demand from now on. Let today be the day the world learns the new rules for dealing with you.

The Butt-Kicking Things I Demand
From Now On

_____

_____

_____

_____

_____

_____

_____

_____

_____

A Wonderful, Amazing, Stupendous, Inspiring, Butt-Kicking Real-Life Story

For as long as she can remember, Elisabeth has always been a performer. Even at the age of four, she knew the exact look, gesture, or act of comedic timing that would leave her audience laughing for days. Every time Elisabeth let her inner actress come out and play, people would unanimously agree that she was meant to be a star.

Elisabeth's parents, refugees who settled in London, refused to enroll her in acting classes. They told Elisabeth she was meant to be a secretary who would bring in a steady paycheck and have a normal, steady life. "Acting," they said, "isn't for people like us."

Elisabeth did her best to find another creative outlet. She learned piano, she sewed, she even cut hair for a time, but her inner actress was never satisfied. It wasn't until Elisabeth reached the absolute lowest point in her life, where she knew she had nothing else to lose, that she was finally able to quiet the "Tsk-tsk" voice of her parents that had remained in her head. Instead of crumpling an advertisement she saw for an acting class, she picked up the phone and enrolled. By the middle of the first class (even though she almost walked out and nearly threw up),

Elisabeth knew she was finally where she belonged. Since that first acting class nearly a decade ago, Elisabeth has become a working actress and the founder and artistic director of her own theatre. She has also never again doubted what she is meant to do.

If Women Ran the World . . . Childhood fantasies wouldn't have to remain in childhood, and they wouldn't be seen as dumb, silly, or foolish either.

A Butt-Kicking Inspiration

Georgia O'Keeffe knew early on that she was born to be an artist. It's amazing to think that a moment of self doubt almost kept some of the most original, exquisite, and beloved images of nature from ever being created.

Her childhood art studies began at a young age and continued after high school at both the Art Institute of Chicago and the Art Students League in New York. Despite winning the League's William Merritt Chase still-life prize in 1908 for her oil painting *Untitled (Dead Rabbit with Copper Pot)*, she stopped painting for several years because she did not believe she could excel in her field.

However, Georgia O'Keeffe's inner artist would not be silenced for long. As time went by, she realized she did not have to conform to the prevalent style of realism that was so popular during her day. She realized she had something to say and that she could do so in her own way. She realized it was time to pick up her paintbrush once more.

When Georgia O'Keeffe made the decision to paint the way *she* wanted to paint, she gave herself the best gift of all: permission to pursue her dreams. With that choice, she also gave a wonderful gift to the world, not just in the beauty of the art she created but also by proving that a dream life really can come true.

Check out: *www.okeeffemuseum.org*

The Butt-Kicking Things I Plan to Do for Myself

What are the things that you most love to do?

What dreams do you want to come true?

What would you include on your light-bulb-dawning, doves-flying-overhead, cue-the-singing angels, I-want-this-more-than-anything list?

If you ran the world, wouldn't every single item you can think of be a regular part of your life right now? Why not run *your* world so these items *are* a part of your life today?

Stop listening to anyone (including yourself) who says you are too young, old, smart, stupid, pretty, ugly, or in some way not right or not enough. You know how good you are at getting sh*t done for other people. Isn't it time you directed your butt-kicking energy toward your happily ever after dreams come true?

Isn't it time you said *yes*! to all the things you have ever planned to do for yourself?

The Butt-Kicking Things I Plan to Do for Myself

_____

_____

_____

_____

_____

_____

_____

_____

_____

A Butt-Kicking Inspiration

Tenley Albright laced up her first pair of ice skates in the early 1940s when she was eight years old, and it wasn't long before she mastered turns and jumps across the ice. Over the next few years, she didn't let anything stand between her and Olympic greatness, be it society's overriding belief that women and athletics did not belong together or a bout with polio when she was eleven. She won the U.S. women's championship when she was sixteen, the silver medal at the 1952 Winter Olympics, and became the first triple crown winner in 1953, winning the world, North American, and U.S. titles. In 1956 she won Olympic gold, skating on an ankle she had gashed to the bone just two weeks earlier.

The following year, Tenley Albright traded her skates for a scalpel, entering Harvard Medical School (one of only six women in her class). She has had a successful career as a surgeon and blood plasma researcher, has served on the Board of Directors of the American Cancer Society, and was Chair of the National Library of Medicine Board of Regents.

Tenley Albright once said, "Don't be so concerned with what other people think, be more concerned with what you think yourself, and what you dare to do."

At a time when society still saw women as either nurses, teachers, or secretaries, Tenley Albright dared to say yes to herself and achieved greatness in not one, but two careers.

Check out:
www.usolympicteam.com
www.achievement.org

If Women Ran the World, Here's What Might Get Done . . .

When it comes down to it, I think it's really quite simple. If women ran the world, then every woman on the planet would be utterly, absolutely, and completely free to live the life of her dreams. Whether that means:

❋ Living in a hut by the Amazon with ten children and no running water or enjoying a house in the suburbs, a dog, and 2.5 kids;

❋ Residing by the beach and writing all day long or, being energized by Wall Street's frenzy; or,

❋ Traveling to every country in Europe or staying close to home

Whatever our heart is longing to do, whatever dream we want for ourselves, no person, law, or societal pressure would ever have the right, ability, or desire to prevent us from pursuing our happily ever after.

I say we start today in our own worlds. We start by giving our dreams and all the things we do for ourselves the same time and attention as all the other things we do.

We start by refusing to let other people, places, or events run us. We start by saying no to what we don't want and yes to what we do. When we get to the point where women everywhere are free to run *their* worlds, we will have reached the point where a woman would have the means, power, and societal approval to actually run the world. What a beautiful day and a beautiful world that will be.

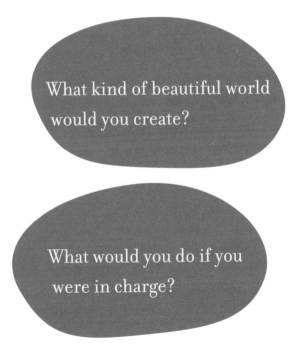

What kind of beautiful world would you create?

What would you do if you were in charge?

If I Ran the World, Here's What
I Would Get Done . . .

_____

_____

_____

_____

_____

_____

_____

_____

_____

Share Your Butt-Kicking Ideas

Share the butt-kicking things you would get done if you ran the world. Log on to *www.ifwomenrantheworld.com* and post all the wonderful, amazing, stupendous, inspiring, butt-kicking ways you would make the world a better place. Whether we use these ideas to bombard our leaders with a butt-kicking action plan or, like the women we are, get sh*t done ourselves, let's create the world we women want, need, and deserve *now*! Let's start today!

Acknowledgments

I am so grateful to the many fabulous women who made
this book possible:

*Jan Johnson, Brenda Knight, Caroline Pincus, Bonni Hamilton and
all the wonderful people at Conari:* Thank you for believing in
this project, for publishing books that make a difference in
people's lives, and for making my publishing dream come true.

Melissa Crew: Thank you for your friendship; your fabulous
salon, Soho by the Sea, in Laguna Beach, California; and all
the inspiration it brought, and for introducing me to Kay.

Kay West: Thank you for your time, your amazing advice,
and for introducing me to the wonderful team at Conari.

Susan Heinz: Thank you for your friendship, your generous
listening, and for your amazing talent for graphics. I am *truly*
grateful to you for everything.

*Judee, Julie, Mom, Alene, Susan, Jennifer, Dawn, Jyn, Marcia,
Judy, Julie, Jan, Hilary*, and *Elisabeth:* Thank you for sharing
your stories with me and for being the amazing women you are.

Jyn, Hilary, Marcia, Loretta, Rebecca, and *Peggy:* Thank you for
all your wonderful feedback and for your generous reading
through the writing of this book.

Dr. Heather Dawn Clark: Thank you for being my mentor, my friend, and my teacher of what's most important, and for always holding this vision for me.

Dr. Jane Claypool: Thank you for giving me a jump start when I needed it the most and for being a true Wise Woman.

Jyn, Elisabeth, Peggy, and *Jon. M*: Thank you for your friendship and for loving me unconditionally. You are four of the most beautiful people I've ever known and I'm so grateful for each of you.

To my family: *Mom*: Thank you for being a living example of a wonderful, amazing, stupendous, inspiring, butt-kicking woman. You inspire me daily. *Dad*: Thank you for always supporting me and allowing me the chance to go for my dreams. *Mindy*: Thank you for being my sister, my friend, and a wonderful, loving, supportive force in my world. *Gary*: Thank you for showing me what life is all about.

And to Jon: Thank you for California. I will always see the beauty you are.

Praise for *If Women Ran the World. . .*

"This is a book of amazing things that women have done in the past, the present, and will continue to do in the future. A must read for all women because we are all incredible!"

— SHANNON HANDWERGER, teacher and mother

"Moms everywhere: grab a glass of wine, lock the bathroom door, and prepare to be inspired because this is definitely a bubble bath book!"

— REBECCA MCLAREN, butt-kicking Mom to three-year-old Jude

"Optimistic and empowering! Filled with stories of women who have chosen to mute naysayers, avert chaos, and stomp out negativity by listening carefully to their inner voices, this book celebrates a myriad of gifts—from eminent accomplishments to tender sacrifices—that our world has received from women."

— AMANDA FORD, author of *Retail Therapy* and *Be True to Yourself*

"Readers will find this book empowers and entertains in equal parts. Shelly Rachanow writes the truth with courage, pizzazz and a straight forward, 'cut to the chase' style that makes this book an absolute must-read. You'll love this unique approach to living life to the fullest."

— DR. JANE CLAYPOOL, author of *Wise Women Don't Worry, Wise Women Don't Sing the Blues*

"A must-have for every woman and for every woman to give to her girlfriends, this little book is filled with inspiration warmly presented with love, respect, and humor! *If Women Ran the World, Sh*t Would Get Done* may be contagious! When I read it, I was at a low point emotionally and to my surprise found myself smiling and even chuckling. I had been gently uplifted."

— DR. HEATHER DAWN CLARK, Pastor, Capistrano Valley Church of Religious Science

"Wow! If any woman wants to get motivated, believe in herself, and do great things, this is the book to read. Dynamic, fun, inspiring, and full of valuable ideas that can turn any woman into whatever she chooses to become. I highly recommend it."

— DR. TERRY COLE-WHITTAKER, author of *What You Think of Me is None of My Business* and *How to Have More in a Have Not World*